THE OFFICIAL
MANCHESTER UNITED®

ENGLISH

BOOK 4

LOUIS FIDGE

Kick-off

The Manchester United books are a fun way to learn and practise your English skills. Each book contains: Theme visits to Manchester United, six Big Matches and a board game!

The 'theme' visits

Learn more about Manchester United and football.

Enjoy the fun activities (*answers on pages 30–31*).

The Big Matches

Learn a new skill.

Practise the skill.

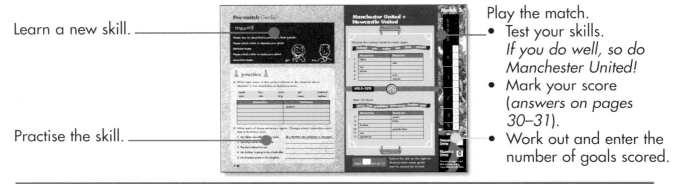

Play the match.
- Test your skills. *If you do well, so do Manchester United!*
- Mark your score (*answers on pages 30–31*).
- Work out and enter the number of goals scored.

After the match: Enter each result on page 28. Work out Manchester United's league position!

The board game

What you need.

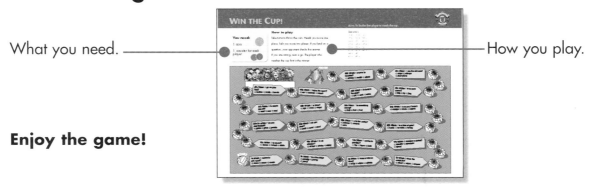

How you play.

Enjoy the game!

Contents

The Megastore MEGA

On a match day, up to 7,000 people may pass through the Megastore at Old Trafford. The Megastore only sells items approved by the Club. There are between 500–600 different things to buy, from pencils to replica kits. You can even buy Manchester United bedspreads and wallpaper and create your own 'Theatre of Dreams' in your bedroom!

The prefix *mega* means 'great' or 'huge'. *Megastore* literally means a 'huge store'!

There are lots of megastars at Manchester United!

2 Draw your favourite megastar (or stick in his photo) and write in his name across the star.

4

1 Art Pack _____
Contains pencils, ruler, glue, markers, paint-brush, sharpener, crayons, eraser and paint.

2 Crest Boot Bag _____
Length: 33 cm, Depth: 15 cm, Height: 12 cm

3 Holdall _____
100% Nylon
Length: 50 cm, Depth: 28 cm, Height: 28 cm

4 Crest and Signature Football
Size 5 _____

5 Old Trafford Wall Clock _____

Here are a few things you can buy.

1 Match the correct description with each item.

a

b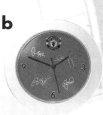

c

d

e

The prefix _uni_ means 'one'. _To unite_ means 'to come together as one'. This is where the word 'United' comes from.

3 All these words have number prefixes. Match up each word with the correct definition.

a | bicycle   three children born to the same mother at the same time

b | centimetre   a hundred years

c | triplets   a two-wheeled vehicle

d | bisect   a three-sided mathematical shape

e | century   to cut into two equal parts

f | triangle   there are a hundred of these in a metre

training

A **suffix** is a group of letters we add to the **end of a word**. A suffix changes the **meaning** of the word or the **job** the word does.

music – musical

practice

A Add the suffix 'al' to each word.

1 music _al_
2 comic ____
3 magic ____
4 person ____
5 coast ____
6 accident ____
7 season ____
8 origin ____
9 topic ____
10 mechanic ____

B Now write the words in alphabetical order.

1 _____
2 _____
3 _____
4 _____
5 _____
6 _____
7 _____
8 _____
9 _____
10 _____

C Choose the correct suffix to complete each word.

1 argu_ment_ (ment/tion)
2 leader_____ (ness/ship)
3 athlet_____ (ary/ic)
4 dark_____ (ate/en)
5 custom_____ (ic/ary)
6 punctu_____ (tion/ate)
7 ill_____ (hood/ness)
8 horr_____ (ify/ise)
9 child_____ (hood/ship)
10 magnet_____ (en/ise)

Manchester United v Leicester City

Choose the correct suffix to complete each word.

1 music_____ (al/ous)

2 fashion_____ (able/ible)

3 educa_____ (ment/tion)

4 amuse_____ (ment/ous)

5 inspec _____ (tion/ment)

6 person_____ (tion/al)

HALF-TIME

Now try these.

7 arrange_____ (tion/ment)

8 comfort_____ (able/ible)

9 sens_____ (able/ible)

10 season_____ (al/ise)

11 ac_____ (ment/tion)

12 invis _____ (able/ible)

Total: [ ] **out of 12**

Colour the bar on the right to find out how many goals you've scored for United.

Training

Professional players have to train hard to keep fit and to sharpen their skills.

Training for the Manchester United players can involve running and sprinting to build up fitness, speed and stamina. Ball skills are practised such as control, tackling, shooting and taking set pieces. Other activities encourage teamwork. The new training centre at Carrington Moss has everything the players need to help them train.

Practise your control and accuracy with this exercise.

2 Work out the words from the co-ordinates given opposite.

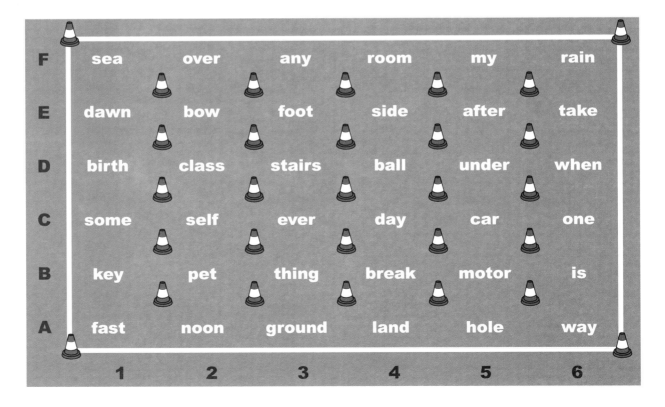

	1	2	3	4	5	6
F	sea	over	any	room	my	rain
E	dawn	bow	foot	side	after	take
D	birth	class	stairs	ball	under	when
C	some	self	ever	day	car	one
B	key	pet	thing	break	motor	is
A	fast	noon	ground	land	hole	way

Practise your passing skills with this exercise.

1 Start with the 'ai' word on the top line. Join it up with the 'ai' word on each line below until you get to the bottom. Do the same for each of the other pairs of vowels, starting with the word on the top line and working your way down.

train	weight	join	build
height	fruit	afraid	noisy
appoint	against	juice	neighbour
spoilt	eighty	guide	entertain
receive	praise	voice	bruise

a 3E + 4D = <u>football</u>

b 4B + 1A = _____

c 5E + 2A = _____

d 6D+ 3C = _____

e 2F + 6E = _____

f 3F + 6A = _____

g 5F + 2C = _____

h 6F + 2E = _____

i 1D+ 4C = _____

j 1F + 4E = _____

9

Pre-match Gender

girl

boy

practice

A Write each noun in the correct column in the chart to show whether it is a masculine or feminine noun.

| queen | boy | uncle | girl | husband |
| aunt | wife | king | niece | nephew |

Masculine	Feminine
	queen

B Write each of these sentences again. Change every masculine noun into a feminine noun.

1 My father was talking to my uncle.   My mother was talking to my aunt.

2 The king looked at the prince.   _____

3 The man helped his son.   _____

4 My brother is going to be a footballer.   _____

5 Mr Lineaker spoke to his daughter.   _____

Manchester United v Newcastle United

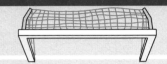

Choose the correct word for each space.

husband   man   mother   girl   uncle   princess

	Masculine	Feminine
1	father	
2		wife
3	boy	
4	prince	
5		aunt
6		woman

HALF-TIME

Now try these.

groom   king   grandfather   sportswoman   daughter   sister

	Masculine	Feminine
7		queen
8		bride
9	brother	
10		grandmother
11	son	
12	sportsman	

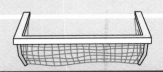

Total: ☐ **out of 12**

Colour the bar on the right to find out how many goals you've scored for United.

GOALS

0	1
	2
	3
	4
1	5
	6
	7
2	8
	9
	10
3	11
4	12

MANCHESTER UNITED ☐

NEWCASTLE UNITED 0

Now turn to page 28 and fill in the score on the Super-League Results Table.

The Kit Manager

We all love watching Manchester United play, but behind the scenes a great number of people who belong to the 'team' help to make it possible.

Albert Morgan, the Kit Manager, has given an interview to the *United News*.

1 Read the report opposite.

Would you make a good Kit Manager?

2 Answer these questions to find out!

1 What is the Kit Manager's name? _____

2 How many work in the Kit Manager's team, including Albert? _____

3 Where does the kit have to be laid out on match days? _____

4 Does Albert need to be around during the match? _____

5 What job has to be done after each match? _____

6 When is the kit washed? _____

7 What are the players' boots washed in? _____

8 How long do the boots take to dry? _____

9 On the coach, what is the kit stored in? _____

10 How many sets of kit does Albert have to take for each

player when United play away? _____

ALBERT MORGAN

Q What exactly do you do, Albert?

A It's my job to make sure that the players, the manager and the coaching staff have all the equipment they need for everyday training as well as their match kit.

Q Do you do this all on your own?

A Oh, no. I have a team of four others working with me.

Q What happens on match days?

A The players' kit has to be laid out in exactly the right place in the dressing room. Each player has his favourite spot. During the game I'm always around in case I'm needed. For example, sometimes a player may need to change the studs on his boots.

Q What about after the game?

A All the kit has to be collected and cleaned. On Monday mornings the laundry room at Old Trafford is very busy. There are many hundreds of pieces of kit to be washed.

Q What happens to the players' boots and trainers?

A I wash them in warm soapy water until they are spotless. They take a couple of days to dry. Then I polish them to keep the leather supple.

Q What is your job when United play away?

A I have to pack everything needed in big metal trunks on wheels to go in the coach. That means three sets of kit for each player. And there are usually about 20 players, so that's a lot of kit!

Score one point for each correct answer then, check your total score on the Kit Manager's Job Rating below.

KIT MANAGER'S JOB RATING

9 - 10	You could be an excellent Kit Manager
6 - 8	You still have a bit to learn
3 - 5	You have a lot to learn!
0 - 2	The Kit Manager's job is not for you!

3 If you could have any job at Manchester United, what would it be?

_____

Pre-match Contractions

training

Sometimes we **shorten** a word by **leaving out** some letters.
We often do it when we are speaking. When we write down
a shortened word, we use an **apostrophe** to show
where letters have been left out.

I've = I have   I've lost my boots!

practice

A Match up each contraction with its longer form.

1	WE'RE		CANNOT
2	WASN'T		DID NOT
3	CAN'T		WE ARE
4	DON'T		IT IS
5	DIDN'T		YOU ARE
6	IT'S		WAS NOT
7	YOU'RE		I AM
8	I'M		DO NOT

B Now try these.

1	WE'LL		WILL NOT
2	THEY'RE		WHERE IS
3	WON'T		WE WILL
4	SHE'S		HERE IS
5	YOU'VE		THEY ARE
6	HERE'S		I HAVE
7	WHERE'S		YOU HAVE
8	I'VE		SHE IS

Manchester United v Aston Villa

Write the longer form of each contraction.

1 can't _____

2 you're _____

3 I'm _____

4 wasn't _____

5 she's _____

6 we're _____

HALF-TIME

Now try these.

7 here's _____

8 don't _____

9 haven't _____

10 I've _____

11 we'll _____

12 it's _____

Total: ⬜ **out of 12**

Colour the bar on the right to find out how many goals you've scored for United.

GOALS

0	1
	2
	3
1	4
	5
	6
2	7
	8
	9
3	10
	11
4	12

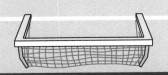

MANCHESTER UNITED ⬜

ASTON VILLA **0**

Now turn to page 28 and fill in the score on the Super-League Results Table.

WIN THE CUP!

You need:

1 coin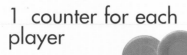

1 counter for each player

How to play

Take turns to throw the coin. Heads you move one place. Tails you move two places. If you land on a question, your opponent checks the answer.

If you are wrong, miss a go. The player who reaches the cup first is the winner.

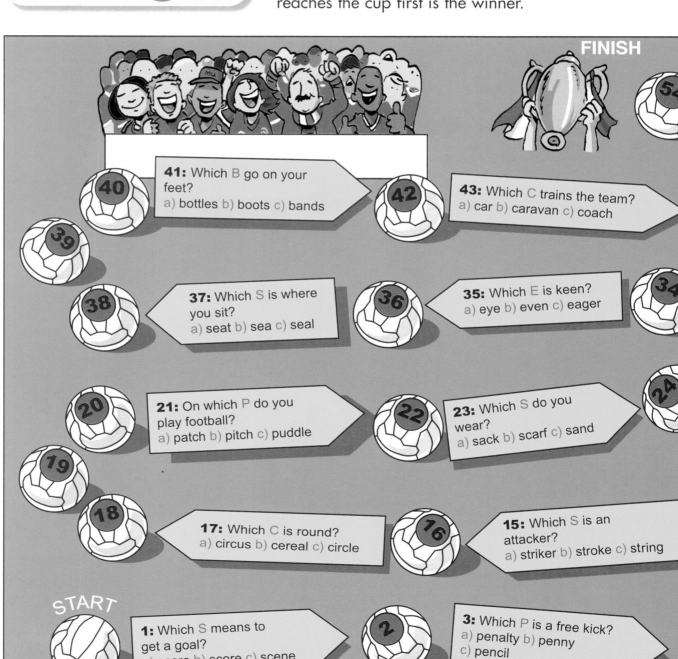

FINISH

54

41: Which B go on your feet?
a) bottles b) boots c) bands

42

43: Which C trains the team?
a) car b) caravan c) coach

40

39

37: Which S is where you sit?
a) seat b) sea c) seal

38

36

35: Which E is keen?
a) eye b) even c) eager

34

21: On which P do you play football?
a) patch b) pitch c) puddle

22

23: Which S do you wear?
a) sack b) scarf c) sand

24

20

19

18

17: Which C is round?
a) circus b) cereal c) circle

16

15: Which S is an attacker?
a) striker b) stroke c) string

START

1: Which S means to get a goal?
a) scare b) score c) scene

2

3: Which P is a free kick?
a) penalty b) penny c) pencil

Aim: To be the first player to reach the cup.

Answers

1 b	3 a	5 c
7 a	11 b	13 c
15 a	17 c	21 b
23 b	25 a	27 b
31 b	33 a	35 c
37 a	41 b	43 c
45 a	47 c	
51 c	53 a	

53: Which A means to surprise?
a) amaze b) assist c) afraid

51: Which C are the winners?
a) chips b) chimps
c) champions

45: Which N is behind the goal?
a) net b) nest c) news

47: Which F is at each corner?
a) fish b) fly c) flag

33: Which F is something wrong?
a) foul b) fool c) fuel

31: Which S is on your boots?
a) stamps b) studs c) stands

Which R runs the match?
eferee b) reserve
ice

27: Which T is a kind of gate?
a) turnip b) turnstile c) turkey

13: Which T means to practise?
a) tea b) team c) train

11: Which S watches a match?
a) speckle b) spectator
c) speed

5: Which W does a referee blow?
a) whip b) whine c) whistle

7: Which C does the crowd do?
a) cheer b) chink c) cheese

Pre-match Diminutives

training

Diminutives are words that suggest something **small**.

A **diminutive** can sometimes be made by adding a **suffix**.

A **diminutive** can sometimes be a **different** word altogether.

duck – duckling

sheep – lamb

practice

A Choose the correct diminutive for each animal.

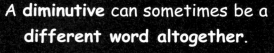

calf   fawn   cub   chick   puppy   lamb   kitten   foal   kid   leveret

1 horse _____foal_____

2 cat _____

3 bear _____

4 hen _____

5 hare _____

6 sheep _____

7 dog _____

8 goat _____

9 deer _____

10 cow _____

B Choose the correct suffix to make a diminutive.

1 gos _ling_ (ling/en)

2 owl_____ (en/et)

3 maid_____ (ling/en)

4 duck_____ (let/ling)

5 book_____ (let/ling)

6 bull_____ (kin/ock)

Manchester United v Fulham

Match up each noun with its correct diminutive.

1	OWL		GOSLING
2	BEAR		BULLOCK
3	GOOSE		OWLET
4	COW		EAGLET
5	BULL		CUB
6	EAGLE		CALF

HALF-TIME

Now try these.

7	DOG		FOAL
8	HEN		KITTEN
9	HORSE		PUPPY
10	SHEEP		PIGLET
11	CAT		LAMB
12	PIG		CHICK

Total: ☐ **out of 12**

Colour the bar on the right to find out how many goals you've scored for United.

0	1
	2
	3
1	4
	5
	6
2	7
	8
	9
3	10
	11
4	12

MANCHESTER UNITED ☐

FULHAM **1**

Now turn to page 28 and fill in the score on the Super-League Results Table.

The Players – Match Day

How do players spend match day? What do they do? Every club has its own routine. Manchester United is no exception.

Read about the players' routine.

1 The boxes opposite show what happens on match days. Unfortunately the events are in the wrong order. Number the boxes to show the correct order.

The team list.

2 Find eleven players' names.

Q	W	B	A	R	T	H	E	Z	E	R	T
Y	U	I	O	P	N	E	V	I	L	L	E
K	E	A	N	E	A	S	D	F	G	H	J
L	Z	X	S	I	L	V	E	S	T	R	E
C	V	B	N	M	Q	S	T	A	M	W	E
R	B	E	C	K	H	A	M	T	Y	U	I
O	P	A	S	D	F	B	U	T	T	G	H
Y	O	R	K	E	J	K	L	Z	X	C	V
B	N	M	Q	W	E	R	T	C	O	L	E
Y	U	I	O	G	I	G	G	S	P	A	S
D	F	S	C	H	O	L	E	S	G	H	J

3 Write the names on your team list.

TEAM LIST
Barthez

a	After the meal, players go to the dressing room for a pre-match meeting with the manager.	
b	Players have a well-deserved bath when the game is over.	
c	After the warm-up, players return to the dressing room and get into their match kit.	
d	Players arrive at Old Trafford for a pre-match meal together.	1
e	Finally, players relax and unwind in the players' lounge before they go home.	
f	Players go out for the big match!	
g	40 minutes before the match, players warm-up on the pitch.	

4 The vowels have been left out of these players' names. Write each name correctly.

PL SCHLS _Paul Scholes_	DVD MY	NCKY BTT
WS BRWN	QNTN FRTNE	NDY CL
DNS RWN	TDDY SHRNGHM	RNNY JHNSN

Pre-match Word Order

training

Sometimes when we **change the order of the words** it changes the **meaning** of the whole sentence.

The player kicked the ball.

The ball kicked the player.

practice

A Arrange these words to make sensible sentences.

1 bark dogs can   Dogs can bark.

2 cat milk my likes

3 footballer the ball the kicks

4 football yesterday played the boy

5 a the crashed into car fence

6 by town went we to bus

B Change around the underlined nouns to make some silly sentences.

1 The <u>referee</u> blew the <u>whistle</u>.   The whistle blew the referee.

2 The <u>lady</u> fried an <u>egg</u>.

3 The <u>boy</u> mowed the <u>lawn</u>.

4 The <u>singer</u> played the <u>guitar</u>.

5 The <u>winger</u> chased the <u>ball</u>.

6 The <u>fireman</u> put out the <u>fire</u>.

Manchester United v Leeds United

Rearrange the words in each sentence so they make sense.

1 The sandwich ate a man.

2 The coach got into the queen.

3 The crown put on his king.

4 The goal scored a striker.

5 The trunk lifted its elephant.

6 Some boots wore the players.

HALF-TIME

Now try these.

7 The runway landed on the plane.

8 The penalty saved the goalkeeper.

9 Stripes have tigers.

10 The television is watching Sam.

11 The bone ate the dog.

12 The piano played the teacher.

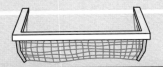

Total: _____ **out of 12**

Colour the bar on the right to find out how many goals you've scored for United.

GOALS

0	1
	2
	3
1	4
	5
	6
2	7
	8
	9
3	10
	11
4	12

MANCHESTER UNITED ☐

LEEDS UNITED **2**

Now turn to page 28 and fill in the score on the Super-League Results Table.

The Match Report

Each game Manchester United play is eagerly reported in the press.

1 Read the report opposite of the game played against Coventry at Old Trafford on 5 February 2000.

Your match report.

2 Write your own match report. It can be about a real match you have seen, or you can make up an imaginary match.

Think of a good headline

Add a photo or drawing from the match

Write an exciting report describing the match

Add the match statistics

MATCH STATISTICS

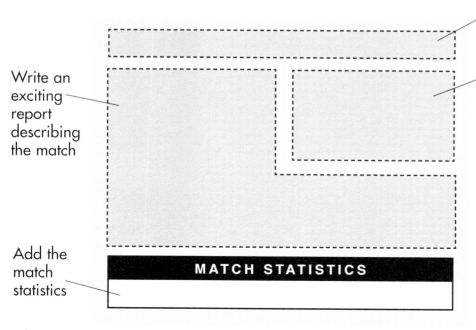

United march on!

Coventry played neat, effective football throughout the match and, in the early stages, United struggled to beat the offside trap. Then, a spectacular strike by Andy Cole in the 40th minute brought this game sizzling to life.

After a long Phil Neville throw-in, Cole darted through the defence and chipped the ball over Hedman into the net. Cole quickly followed this up with a close-range header, from a Beckham free kick.

Coventry refused to cave in. The Belgian, Roussel, pulled one back for the visitors with a lovely near-post drive. After 77 minutes Paul Scholes made the score 3–1. Then, in the last minute of the game, Roussel scored his second for Coventry.

The final result was a true reflection of the closeness of the contest.

MATCH STATISTICS

Manchester United 3
Cole 40, 55, Scholes 77
Coventry 2
Roussel 65, 90

Attendance 61,380

MATCH STATISTICS

Pre-match Common Letter Strings

training

Letter strings are groups of letters which make up part of a word. Some letter strings are very **common** – but they do not always make the same sound!

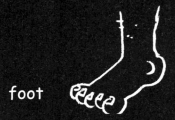

foot

boot

practice

A Match up and write the pairs of words that contain the same letter strings.

1	COUGH	ALLOW
2	POST	COULD
3	GROW	TOUGH
4	SHOULDER	BONE
5	LOOK	COST
6	GONE	SOON

_____

_____

cough   tough

_____

_____

_____

B Make up some sentences using each pair of words.

1	MOTH	MOTHER
2	OFFICE	NICE
3	GLOVE	MOVE
4	SNOW	COW
5	CASE	VASE
6	WALLET	MALLET

My mother was scared of the moth.

_____

_____

_____

_____

Manchester United v Everton

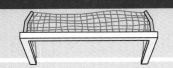

Underline the odd word out in each set.

1	tough	<u>cough</u>	enough
2	five	hive	give
3	have	wave	gave
4	lost	cost	post
5	how	glow	now
6	love	glove	move

HALF-TIME

Now try these.

7	height	eight	weight
8	bear	near	fear
9	good	wood	blood
10	stone	gone	bone
11	caught	taught	laugh
12	wallet	mallet	pallet

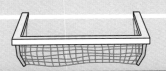

Total: ☐ **out of 12**

Colour the bar on the right to find out how many goals you've scored for United.

GOALS

0	1
	2
	3
1	4
	5
	6
2	7
	8
	9
3	10
	11
4	12

MANCHESTER UNITED ☐

EVERTON 1

Now turn to page 28 and fill in the score on the Super-League Results Table.

Super-League Results

MATCH 1

Man Utd	☐	Leicester City	**3**
Everton	**4**	Aston Villa	**2**
Newcastle	**2**	Leeds Utd	**2**

MATCH 2

Man Utd	☐	Newcastle	**0**
Aston Villa	**2**	Leicester City	**1**
Everton	**2**	Fulham	**2**

MATCH 3

Aston Villa	**0**	Man Utd	☐
Newcastle	**5**	Leicester City	**0**
Leeds Utd	**3**	Fulham	**2**

MATCH 4

Fulham	**1**	Man Utd	☐
Aston Villa	**2**	Newcastle	**3**
Everton	**0**	Leeds Utd	**3**

MATCH 5

Leeds Utd	**2**	Man Utd	☐
Fulham	**1**	Newcastle	**1**
Everton	**2**	Leicester City	**1**

MATCH 6

Man Utd	☐	Everton	**1**
Leicester City	**2**	Leeds Utd	**0**
Aston Villa	**1**	Fulham	**3**

MATCH 7

Fulham	**2**	Leicester City	**3**
Aston Villa	**3**	Leeds Utd	**3**
Everton	**0**	Newcastle	**1**

Super-League Tables

Enter the score for each match.

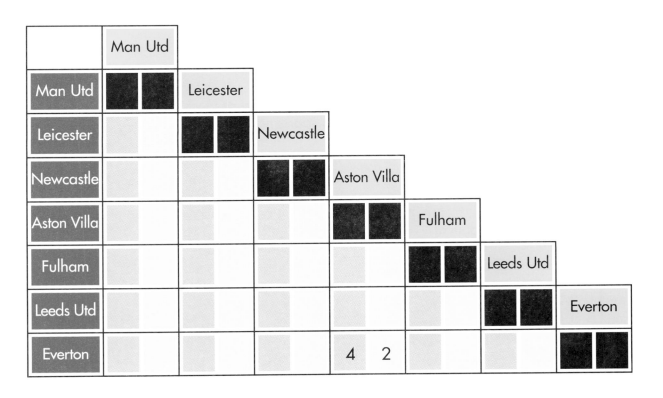

Complete the league table when all the matches are finished.

Win   3 pts   Draw   1 pt   Lose   0 pts

Team	Played	Won	Drew	Lost	For	Against	Goal diff	Points
Man Utd	6							
Leicester	6							
Newcastle	6							
Aston Villa	6							
Fulham	6							
Leeds Utd	6							
Everton	6							

Champions _____   Runners-up _____

The Megastore 4–5
1 artpack – **c**   boot bag – **d**   holdall – **a**
football – **e**   wall clock – **b**
2 (open)
3 a bicycle – a two-wheeled vehicle
b centimetre – there are a hundred of these
in a metre
c triplets – three children born to the same
mother at the same time
d bisect – to cut into two equal parts
e century – a hundred years
f triangle – a three-sided mathematical shape

Match 1 Suffixes 6–7

Pre-Match
A 1 musical **2** comical **3** magical
4 personal **5** coastal **6** accidental
7 seasonal **8** original **9** topical
10 mechanical
B 1 accidental **2** coastal **3** comical
4 magical **5** mechanical **6** musical
7 original **8** personal **9** seasonal
10 topical
C 1 argument **2** leadership **3** athletic
4 darken **5** customary **6** punctuate
7 illness **8** horrify **9** childhood
10 magnetise

The Match
1 musical **2** fashionable **3** education
4 amusement **5** inspection **6** personal
7 arrangement **8** comfortable **9** sensible
10 seasonal **11** action **12** invisible

Training 8–9
1 train – afraid – against – entertain – praise
weight – height – neighbour – eighty –
receive
join – noisy – appoint – spoilt – voice
build – fruit – juice – guide – bruise
2 a football **b** breakfast **c** afternoon
d whenever **e** overtake **f** anyway
g myself **h** rainbow **i** birthday
j seaside

Match 2 Gender 10–11

Pre-match
A masculine – boy, uncle, husband, king,
nephew
feminine – queen, girl, aunt, wife, niece

B 1 My mother was talking to my aunt.
2 The queen looked at the princess.
3 The woman helped her daughter.
4 My sister is going to be a footballer.
5 Mrs Lineaker spoke to her daughter.

The Match
1 father – mother **2** husband – wife
3 boy – girl **4** prince – princess
5 uncle – aunt **6** man – woman
7 king – queen **8** groom – bride
9 brother – sister
10 grandfather – grandmother
11 son – daughter
12 sportsman – sportswoman

The Kit Manager 12–13
1 (open)
2 1 Albert Morgan 2 five 3 in exactly the
right place in the dressing room 4 yes
5 The kit has to be collected and cleaned.
6 Monday mornings 7 warm soapy water
8 two days 9 big metal trunks on wheels
10 three
3 (open)

Match 3 Contractions 14–15
Pre-match
A 1 we're – we are **2** wasn't – was not
3 can't – cannot **4** don't – do not
5 didn't – did not **6** it's – it is
7 you're – you are **8** I'm – I am
B 1 we'll – we will **2** they're – they are
3 won't – will not **4** she's – she is
5 you've – you have **6** here's – here is
7 where's – where is **8** I've – I have

The Match
1 can't – cannot **2** you're – you are
3 I'm – I am **4** wasn't – was not
5 she's – she is **6** we're – we are
7 here's – here is **8** don't – do not
9 haven't – have not **10** I've – I have
11 we'll – we will **12** it's – it is

Match 4 Diminutives 18–19
Pre-match
A 1 foal **2** kitten **3** cub **4** chick **5** leveret **6**
lamb **7** puppy **8** kid **9** fawn **10** calf
B 1 gosling **2** owlet **3** maiden **4** duckling
5 booklet **6** bullock

The Match

1 owl – owlet **2** bear – cub
3 goose – gosling **4** cow – calf
5 bull – bullock **6** eagle – eaglet
7 dog – puppy **8** hen – chick
9 horse – foal **10** sheep – lamb
11 cat – kitten **12** pig – piglet

The Players – Match Day 20–21

1 Players arrive at Old Trafford for a pre-match meal together.
After the meal, players go to the dressing room for a pre-match meeting with the manager.
40 minutes before the match, players warm-up on the pitch.
After the warm-up, players return to the dressing room and get into their match kit.
Players go out for the big match!
Players have a well-deserved bath when the game is over.
Finally, players relax and unwind in the players' lounge before they go home.
2–3 Barthez, Neville, Keane, Silvestre, Stam, Beckham, Butt, Yorke, Cole, Giggs, Scholes
4 Paul Scholes, David May, Nicky Butt, Wes Brown, Quinton Fortune, Andy Cole, Denis Irwin, Teddy Sheringham, Ronny Johnsen

Match 5 Word Order 22–23

Pre-Match
Answers may differ slightly from those given.
A 1 Dogs can bark. **2** My cat likes milk.
   3 The footballer kicks the ball.
   4 Yesterday the boy played football.
   5 The car crashed into a fence.
   6 We went to town by bus.
B 1 The whistle blew the referee.
   2 An egg fried the lady.
   3 The lawn mowed the boy.
   4 The guitar played the singer.
   5 The ball chased the winger.
   6 The fire put out the fireman.

The Match
   1 The man ate a sandwich.
   2 The queen got into the coach.
   3 The king put on his crown.
   4 The striker scored a goal.
   5 The elephant lifted its trunk.
   6 The players wore some boots.

7 The plane landed on the runway.
8 The goalkeeper saved the penalty.
9 Tigers have stripes.
10 Sam is watching the television.
11 The dog ate the bone.
12 The teacher played the piano.

The Match Report 24–25

1, 2 (open)

Match 6 Common Letter Strings 26–27

Pre-Match
A 1 cough – tough **2** post – cost
   3 grow – allow **4** shoulder – could
   5 look – soon **6** gone – bone
B 1–6 (open)

The Match
1 cough **2** give **3** have **4** post **5** glow
6 move **7** height **8** bear **9** blood **10** gone
11 laugh **12** wallet

Collect the set

**Each book introduces new skills and harder challenges.
Collect all 16 and be an English and Maths champion.**

Manchester United English   Louis Fidge

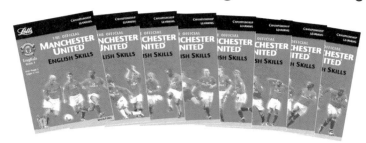

Manchester United Maths   Paul Broadbent

**For all the latest
news,
views and
information on**

MANCHESTER UNITED

*visit the official
Manchester United
website:*

www.manutd.com

Manchester United Plc, Sir Matt Busby Way, Old Trafford, Manchester M16 0RA

**Letts Educational, Aldine House, Aldine Place, London W12 8AW
Tel: 020 8740 2266 Fax: 020 8743 8451 E-mail: mail@lettsed.co.uk
Website: www.letts-education.com**

Every effort has been made to trace copyright holders and obtain their permission for the use of copyright material. The authors and publishers will gladly receive information enabling them to rectify any error or omission in subsequent editions.

All facts are correct at time of going to press.

Published 2000
Text © Letts Educational Ltd. Published under licence from Manchester United Football Club, Video Collection International Limited and Carlton Books Limited. All Trade Marks related to Manchester United Football Club are used with the permission of Manchester United Football Club, Video Collection International Limited and Carlton Books Limited.
Author: Louis Fidge
Editorial and Design: Moondisks Ltd, Cambridge
Illustrations: Joel Morris
Our thanks to Mark Wylie (MUFC museum curator) and John Peters (MUFC official photographer) for supplying material and their cooperation in the production of these books.

British Library Cataloguing in Publication Data
A CIP record for this book is available from the British Library.

ISBN 1-85805-870-8

Printed in the UK.

Letts Educational Limited is a member of Granada Learning Limited, part of the Granada Media Group.